I'M LEARNING, LORD, BUT I STILL NEED HELP

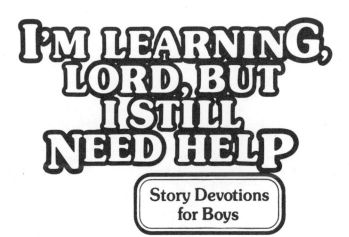

Story Devotions for Boys

NATE AASENG

AUGSBURG Publishing House • Minneapolis

I'M LEARNING, LORD, BUT I STILL NEED HELP

MANUFACTURED IN THE UNITED STATES OF AMERICA

Contents

About This Book

This book is a book of story problems. It isn't a math book, but a group of problems surrounded by real-life settings in which you might find them. The problems are wrapped up in noisy gyms, annoying little brothers, and warm summer days. The answers are sometimes clouded by the presence of friends and even your own feelings.

It's just like doing math at school. It wasn't too hard to figure out problems when they were all set up for you. All you had to do was plug in the formula and you get the answer. Then they hit you with the story problems. Now the numbers are buried in a lot of other information. On some of the trickier ones, they include information that you don't even need.

Growing up works the same way. At first the questions are all set up and the answers come easily: obey the Commandments, do good to others, give thanks to God for what you have.

That's fine until the real-life problems come. Suddenly you have to work harder to find the answers. There are choices to be made about how important God, church, school, parents, sports, girls, and other things really are. There are tough decisions about how to get along with friends and people you don't want as friends. On top of that, you feel pressure from the world around you to do things you don't think you should.

You're learning, but some of the story problems you run into are real brain teasers. You could think about them for weeks without coming up with the answers. Those are the times when you really feel you could use some help. You need to know that someone is on your side, that it isn't just you facing life all by yourself.

At those times, God can help in many ways. Sometimes just a smile from someone you don't know can point you in the right direction. Parents, brothers, sisters, and friends can help encourage you. You can also get strength and insight from talking directly to God in prayer. Remembering that he is there can help you with even the toughest problems.

My thanks to the real-life boys who, through their own actions, provided stories for this book. Your concerns may not always be the same as theirs, but since they come from all over, farms, cities, small towns, and suburbs, I hope you can see some of your own life in theirs. Perhaps by practicing on their problems, and remembering where to get help, you can learn more about how to solve your own problems.

Hold All Calls!

Jerome could still hear them laughing at him. He barely noticed the pain from his bruised leg anymore, but the gravy stains on his white pants kept reminding him of what had happened that noon. He had been carrying his lunch tray and looking to see where his friends were sitting. Just as he had spotted them, his foot slipped on some grease. He had fallen heavily. His lunch had spilled all over himself and the floor. Nearly everyone in the lunchroom had stood and cheered. "Even my friends were laughing," he thought as he rubbed at the stain.

"Jerome." He sat up with a start. His teacher, Mrs. Anderson, was leaning forward on her elbows at her desk. "Would you read the next part for us?" she asked. Jerome searched his literature book for a clue as to where to begin. A quick glance at Freddie Wells' book told him he wasn't even on the right page. He could feel a rush of blood starting to turn his face red.

"You haven't been paying attention, have you?" sighed Mrs. Anderson. "I'm afraid we'll have to talk about that after school."

When Jerome got home, he was in no mood to be pleasant. "Why do rotten things always happen to me?" he mumbled through supper.

"It sounds as though you've had a rough day," said his mother. "By the way, Darrel called. He wants you to help him plan the Easter breakfast."

Jerome frowned and said nothing. After supper he went into the TV room and closed the door behind him. Minutes later his dad saw him stomp angrily out of the room.

"Wouldn't you know?" said Jerome. "My show isn't on. Some special on hunger or something. I must be the most unlucky person in the world. I don't know why I even try anymore."

"I'll tell you what," said his dad. "I'll be your secretary and you can take the weekend off. You see, when my boss at work doesn't want to be bothered, he has his secretary hold all his calls. I'll do that for you. You can stay in the house and I'll see to it that no one bugs you."

"Really?" asked Jerome. "Now that's an idea I like!"

On Saturday, Jerome felt important. He put on a stack of records and lay back on a fluffed-up pillow. After awhile he pulled out his aircraft carrier model. Using a toothpick, he painted the guns, the tower, and the planes. After lunch, he read for a while and then went down to see what was on TV. Once he

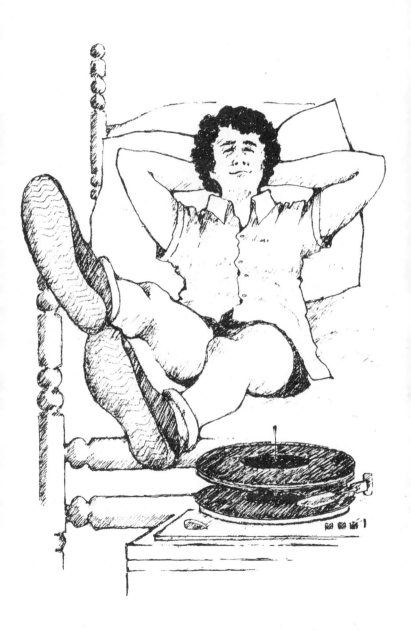

heard the doorbell, and later the phone rang. Jerome looked up at the clock. Not quite four o'clock. Still a long time until supper. The day wasn't much fun anymore. Jerome had to admit he was bored.

As he walked into the dining room, his dad looked up. "Well, sir, are you enjoying your day?" asked his dad.

Jerome did not want to hurt his dad's feelings, but finally he had to shake his head. "What was that phone call about?" he asked.

"It was Joe. He didn't say what he wanted." He put down his pen. "What's wrong? I thought you were looking forward to this day."

"I was."

"But nothing bad has happened to you all day."

"For the last couple hours, nothing *at all* has happened," said Jerome.

Dad smiled. "Was today any different from being grounded?"

Jerome's eyes widened. "No, I guess not. And to think I was looking forward to it. I suppose you knew that I wouldn't like today."

"I wasn't sure. In fact I was afraid the whole idea of playing secretary was stupid. That's often the way my plans end up."

"You know how I feel then, don't you?" asked Jerome.

"I think I do," said Dad. "We all have days when everything goes great and days when nothing works for us. It's not always our fault either."

"I guess today shows that the only way to miss the bad days is to miss the good days too," replied Je-

12

rome. "So how does that help me get through a day like yesterday?"

"You don't have to face troubles alone. That's what friends and family are for. God can be an even better help. But he doesn't want you to miss out on life by hiding. God doesn't hold all calls for you or anyone else."

Jerome looked at the floor. "You know, when I thought about it last night, I knew what I said was dumb. Who else could watch a few minutes of poor, hungry people on TV and still feel sorry for himself?"

"That's the trouble with the 'Always me' feeling. We look at ourselves and our problems so much we don't see others who need our help."

"Well, I'm going to go see what Joe wanted," said Jerome, putting on his jacket. "That is, if I don't break a leg on the way over," he smiled.

> And let us not grow weary in
> well-doing, for in due season we
> shall reap, if we do not lose heart.
> Galatians 6:9

Lord, I'm probably not the first person who wished that life was perfect, at least perfect for myself. But I'm not the only one living here in this world either. I guess it would be pretty dull if I was. When I really think about it, I'm glad you're in charge of the world. Help me to bounce back when things get me down.

Favorite Horses

"Kathy, get away from my horse!"

"Blackie isn't your horse, Andy. He's Mr. Gantner's. Anyway, you got to ride him yesterday. I got here first today!"

"Forget it!" he snapped. "You just picked him because you knew he was my favorite."

"Now don't go scarin' the horses," said Mr. Gantner. "They get skittish when people carry on like that around them." He carried a polished leather saddle towards Blackie's stall. "Andy, why don't you let your little sister ride Blackie? You can take Ransom."

Andy gave his sister one last disgusted stare and trudged to Ransom's stall. He wasn't thinking how grateful he should be to the Gantners for even letting him ride. He was still too angry at Kathy for that. The Gantners were old friends of his parents.

This week the whole family was visiting the Gantners and their old riding stable. The stable wasn't much to look at—it used to be a tobacco shed. There weren't more than two or three spots in it where you could stand in a rain storm and not get wet.

Andy pulled extra hard on Ransom's saddle cinch to make sure it was on tight. Then he hunted for a bridle.

"Ready to go?" called Mr. Gantner. "Kathy and I are all saddled up."

"Sure. Come on, Ransom." As he led the horse out of the stall, Andy stayed well away from the horse's feet. Ransom was known to step on any stray feet he could reach.

Though tired and dirty from his day's work, Mr. Gantner had agreed to take Andy and Kathy on an evening trail ride. They rode along a wooded trail that wound up a steep hill. At the top the trail opened up into a meadow. From there it was easy to see how the ridges cut sharply down into the valley where the Gantners lived. The sun was sliding down behind the highest ridge to the west. It cast a soft orange light that made the valley seem even more dreamy and beautiful than usual. Trotting through the fresh evening air almost made Andy forget that his sister was on Blackie. Almost. Kathy could not keep Blackie from stopping to munch on clover, so the other horses had to slow to a walk.

Their parents met them when they reached the bottom of the trail. They helped them walk the horses into the stable. "How was the ride?" asked Mom.

"Great!" said Kathy, and she told about the sunset

and ride through the clover-filled meadow. Just rubbing it in, thought Andy.

"Do you mind if we greenhorns ride with you tomorrow?" asked Dad.

"Can we leave Kathy behind?" asked Andy. "We always have to go so slow because of her."

"Is something the matter between you two?"

"No, Dad," sighed Andy. Mr. Gantner felt awkward. The two children had been fighting most of the day, and he didn't really know what to do about it.

"I've got some news that will brighten your day tomorrow," he said. "I've got a new recruit comin' in the morning. His name's Pharaoh. He's a nice-looking buckskin horse."

"Can I ride him first?" begged Kathy.

"Sure, you get to do everything first. I'm surprised you let anyone else ride with you," muttered Andy.

"Isn't that enough fighting for one day?" asked Mom.

"No reason to fight anyway," said Mr. Gantner, letting the horses out for the evening. "We'll have to let Pharaoh get used to his new pals before we let anyone ride him."

"Can't I ride him just once?" pleaded Kathy.

"Quit being a brat," scolded Andy.

Mr. Gantner closed the gate behind him as they walked toward the house. "No, I'm afraid life is pretty rough for a new horse. We'll leave him be. If you want to see him brought in tomorrow, you'll have to be up early. Join me around seven by the side pasture."

As Mr. Gantner left, Dad turned to Andy and Kathy. "If all you're going to do is fight with each other all day, you could just as well do that at home."

"Sorry," said Andy. "Getting along isn't always easy."

The next morning Andy woke up to a low, rumbling sound. At first he paid no attention to it. Suddenly he sat up. "That's a truck! It must be the new horse!" He jumped out of bed and pulled on his clothes. He bounced down the steps two at a time and raced out the back door. The grassy path had his feet soaked with dew by the time he reached the others. He was the last of the family to get there.

"Just in time, Andy. Here he comes," said Mom. The horse looked almost golden as it backed out of the trailer. When the head finally appeared, Andy could see the horse had a white mane and face. It strained at its halter, eyes wide in fear.

"Wow! I think I like that one as much as Blackie," said Andy.

Mr. Gantner patted the horse and spoke to it in low tones until it quieted down. Andy could see that the other horses were inching closer to the gate trying to get a closer look at the new arrival. Mr. Gantner shooed them away with his hand and opened the door.

"Good luck, pardner. You're going to need it," he said. He pulled the creaky gate shut behind the horse.

"Why did you wish him good luck, Mr. Gantner?" asked Kathy.

"Watch," was all he answered. For a few minutes the new horse paced nervously along the fence. Gradually several of the other horses came close to him. Pharaoh backed off, staring at them. Suddenly

17

Blackie plunged in after Pharaoh with his teeth. Both horses gave out high, piercing whinnies. Pharaoh turned and kicked Blackie who twisted around and tried to do the same to Pharaoh.

"Why are they fighting?" asked Andy.

"That's what usually happens with a new horse. It takes horses awhile to get used to each other," said Mr. Gantner. "I suppose they want to show each other who's boss. And they get angry because they think other horses will get in their way."

"Blackie, please stay away from Pharaoh," said Kathy. But a second quick clash between the horses was so fierce and sudden it made her jump.

"I don't even like to watch," said Andy. "It wouldn't even be so bad if they weren't my favorite horses. Look at that! They're being just awful to each other." Blackie led two other horses in a charge that sent Pharaoh bucking into a corner by the fence.

"Now you know how your father and I feel," said Mom softly.

Kathy and Andy both turned. "Oh, you mean 'cause we fight," said Kathy.

"Yes," replied Mom. "You are our favorite people. And you're so much more valuable to us than the horses are to you. When you can't get along it makes us feel terrible."

"As you said yourself, Andy, it's not much fun to watch," said Dad.

"I guess we were kind of being like Blackie and Pharaoh," said Andy. "We were being pretty selfish. Every time we got in each other's way we started fighting."

18

"Will Blackie and Pharaoh always fight?" wondered Kathy.

"No," replied Mr. Gantner. "After a few days or maybe a couple of weeks they'll learn to get along. Each will find out that the other really isn't as terrible as he thought."

"Why does it take us so much longer than horses?" asked Andy.

"Often it takes adults even longer than kids," said Dad. "Just one look at the newspaper shows how hard it is for them to get along. War, crime, and arguments all the time."

"Since God loves us so much, I bet that makes him just sick to watch those things happen too," said Andy.

Mr. Gantner was smiling as he leaned against the knobby fence. "The funny thing about it is that the horses have all they need. If they weren't so busy kicking each other, they could be having fun running around and eating their fill."

Andy laughed. "I'll bet we would be having a much better time this week if we weren't so busy being selfish."

"From now on let's try to find out just how good a time we *can* have," suggested Dad.

"Yeah," said Kathy. "We can do better than a couple of horses."

> He who loves his brother abides
> in the light, and in it there is no
> cause for stumbling.
>
> 1 John 2:10

19

I know it hurts when we don't get along. It hurts you, our parents, and us. Help us to remember that when people, especially family, get in my way, it's because I haven't left room for them in my heart.

Picking on Leon

"I sure am glad I'm not Leon!" Robbie could tell it was going to be a rough day for Leon. The second their teacher turned his back, the boy sitting behind Leon had reached down and grabbed Leon's books. Robbie helped pass the books to the back of the room where they were hidden in the wastebasket under the pencil sharpener.

Leon was always getting picked on. It had been going on ever since he moved to town early the year before. Not that he was so different from everyone else. He had a funny, whiney voice, and he wasn't very coordinated, but he was a fairly good student and was always friendly. Maybe his problem was that he tried *too* hard to be friendly. "Doesn't he ever keep quiet?" Robbie had asked one of his friends. "He always acts like he's my best buddy."

"Ow!" cried Leon. All the boys and girls near the

back of the room tried to hold back giggles. Tom Johnson was an expert at shooting paper clips.

"What's going on in here?" demanded Mr. Willis. The giggles stopped.

"Someone hit me with something," said Leon. "They got me right here in the back. It hurts."

Robbie rolled his eyes in impatience. If Leon would not make such a big deal out of it, no one would pick on him. Half the fun was seeing him get all riled up. Robbie didn't listen to Mr. Willis' stern lecture. He had heard the speech before. Robbie knew it wasn't right to give Leon such a bad time. When he was feeling guiltiest about it he would pretend not to notice when his friends played tricks on Leon. But it was strange how it made everyone else feel like part of a close group when they all ganged up on one person. Anytime you wanted someone on your side or wanted to get a laugh, all you had to do was pick on Leon. Besides, Robbie was going to be very careful that he didn't get singled out like Leon.

As Robbie left class, he saw some of his friends huddled together in the middle of the hall. Robbie leaned his head in to catch what they were saying. "Let's throw him in the girls' bathroom," said one. Even Robbie smiled at the thought. The four of them pushed through the crowded hall to catch up with Leon. Just as he passed the girls' bathroom, three pairs of arms grabbed him. Robbie held back nervously.

"Hey! Cut it out!" started Leon. But before he could say any more he was shoved backward through the door. Robbie could hear some girls' screams and the hallway filled with laughter.

Robbie was still smiling when Leon reappeared with his shirttails hanging out. Leon began to gather up his books with covers scuffed up from being thrown around. Robbie wondered how it must feel to be in Leon's place. Leon was very near crying, but he refused to let anyone see him in tears. The hall was nearly empty when Leon got his things back in order. He looked around as if searching for someone he could at least talk to. Then he shuffled slowly down the hall.

It began to bother Robbie. Even in bed that night he lay awake thinking about Leon. "He must spend his whole life hating every new day that he wakes up," thought Robbie. "I wish I were bigger and stronger or more popular. Then I could watch out for people like Leon. It would be so much easier on everyone."

Turning over on his back, he prayed out loud. "Dear God, please watch over Leon. You are strong enough to keep him from any more trouble. And find a friend for him. Amen."

The next day Robbie saw Leon standing in the hall trying to get his jacket zipper unstuck. When he finally worked it free he looked up and saw Robbie staring at him. He automatically backed against the wall and covered his books with both hands. "Hi," he said uncertainly.

Robbie was about to answer when he saw his friends bounding down the stairway.

"Hey, Robbie!" they shouted. "Looks like you

found Leon. Have you ever seen anyone who was more of a loser than Leon?"

Robbie panicked. "No," he said, smiling at them. "I'll see you guys later, I have to get to class early." He had to leave fast. He could not stand to see what Leon's hopeful eyes looked like now. It didn't make him feel any better when he had to walk by Leon's table at lunchtime. Leon sat alone in the center of the lunchroom. Nobody would even sit at the same table. Leon ate a sandwich hurriedly and threw the rest of his lunch away. Then he disappeared back into the hall.

Robbie did not feel much like going to the midweek service at church that night. He was disappointed that God wasn't answering his prayer. Even worse, he was disappointed at himself. He sat glumly in the pew next to his parents. It didn't feel right to sing, so he drummed his fingers gently on the hymnal during the hymn.

He did feel like listening. Somehow it seemed easier to do when darkness was all that showed through the side windows of the church and his mind was not filled with thoughts of what he was going to do that day as it usually was on Sunday morning.

A woman who looked familiar read the Bible passage. She told about how Jesus was captured and how Peter struck out with his sword. Robbie always felt bad at hearing those verses. He wished Jesus would have let Peter help. With God's help it would have been so easy to wipe out all their enemies.

But the sermon was saying something different. Jesus didn't come to beat up people. He didn't come to save himself, or even to save someone like Leon from being picked on. In a way, Robbie thought, Jesus was a lot like Leon. In fact he was picked on much worse. They shoved him around and laughed at him. They even killed him.

"He did it for you," the pastor was saying. Jesus was the one who was picked on so the rest of us could live. All the sins of the world were heaped on him.

"My prayer wasn't such a good one," thought Robbie. "It was like Peter trying to fight with his sword. If we can be big and powerful we are willing to help Jesus crush the bad guys. But Jesus knew that only his suffering would make up for our wrongs. Then we make him pay the price all alone."

Robbie remembered Leon's pleading, hopeful eyes that never found anything but tormentors. He was paying the price for everyone else's good time. Jesus' eyes must have looked the same, especially when his disciples denied they even knew him.

Wasn't there some Bible verse that said if you help the least of God's children you were helping him? As he passed the offering plate, Robbie decided there was only one thing to do. Maybe he was crazy for trying it, but he was feeling that a lot had been done for him and he had not shown much gratitude. It was time he did something in return.

At school the next day, Robbie waited by the lunchroom door. His brown bag was growing limp and wet from his sweating palms. He had told his friends that morning what he thought he should do. To his surprise, one of his friends agreed that Leon deserved a break. His other friends said nothing. But Robbie could tell by their silence that they were wondering if it would be safe. Would they start getting picked on too?

Then he saw Leon walking alone. Leon stayed close to the pink tile wall, especially when he heard a group of boys laughing behind him. Robbie took a deep breath. "Leon," he called.

Leon stopped and looked around quickly. "Oh, hi, Robbie," he said, his stiffened shoulders relaxing slightly. Robbie could tell by his smile that Leon had forgotten yesterday's insult.

"Why don't you sit with us today?" said Robbie. "We're over by the window."

"Lead the way," answered Leon. Instead of his usual put-on smile, Leon's lips were pursed as he tried to hold back a more genuine one. Robbie could not help but notice one empty table they passed. All 10 chairs were still neatly arranged, pushed in against a shiny tabletop streaked with dried cleanser. It was Leon's table. "An empty table never looked so good," thought Robbie as they brushed past it.

> Surely he has borne our griefs
> and carried our sorrows.
>
> Isaiah 53:4

You went through a lot for me, Jesus. Your love for me must be stronger than anything I can understand. I want to thank you. I need to thank you, in ways that show.

Buy Now, Pay Later

Steve was expecting the beach to be crowded on such a hot day, but this was ridiculous. Colorful beach blankets were spread like a mosaic tile all across the sand. The roped-in swimming area was alive with wet heads, waving arms, splashing water, shouts, and laughter.

Steve dropped his towel up on the grass and threaded his way through the blankets. He had only walked three blocks from his home and already sweat was sliding down, stinging his eyes. Most of the kids he knew were already in the water. He spotted his best friend, John, diving near the orange rope. There was no sense trying to yell to him with all that racket, so Steve waded in, staying clear of splash fights.

John was so busy diving that he wasn't paying attention to anything else. Steve decided to give him a surprise greeting. He crouched low until his chin was touching the water and crept closer. Then he jumped up, grabbed John's shoulders, and pulled him under the water. Smiling, he swam away through a crowd of girls before John could get him back.

But John had just been taking a deep breath for another dive when Steve dunked him. He came up coughing and choking so hard that Steve was afraid he might be in trouble. When John finally cleared himself of the water he had swallowed, he whirled around with an angry scowl.

"Oh, no! Now he's really going to be mad," thought Steve, and he swam underwater towards the shore. He kept his eyes open to make sure he didn't bump into any legs. For about a minute he hid behind some smaller boys who were seeing how high out of the water they could jump. Then he got up and walked out toward John.

"Hi, John. Sorry I'm late," he called.

"Who pulled me under?" demanded John.

"When? Come on, I just got here."

"Are you sure you didn't dunk me, Steve Francis?"

"I don't know anything about it," answered Steve.

John could not wear his glasses in the water, so he had a hard time seeing who else was around. He squinted until he picked up the blurred form of someone he knew. "I know who it was. That Brad Davis."

"Why don't you just forget it," said Steve, trying to lead him back to the orange rope. "What were you diving for?"

John brushed him away. "You're real tough, Da-

28

vis!" he sneered. "Run away and hide after you dunk me. Sissy!" Steve wished he could keep John quiet. Brad was another good friend. This thing had already gone too far and looked like it would get worse. But Steve didn't want John mad at *him*, and it was getting too late for an easy explanation anyway.

"What are you crying about now?" shouted Brad. The more John accused him, the angrier Brad became. It took a stern warning from the lifeguard before the two backed away from each other. Steve followed John back to the beach. John stomped over to his towel and shook the sand out with an extra snap.

"Maybe he really didn't do it," insisted Steve. "Can't you let it go, just once?" But John didn't say anything more on the way home.

After that, Brad and John avoided each other as they would a radiation leak. Brad was furious at being called names when he hadn't done anything. John refused to believe Brad. Steve was the most miserable. He missed being able to ride bikes with the two of them. One wouldn't come over to the park to throw the football around if the other was there. And even though the muggy weather lasted through the week, neither of Steve's friends would go down to the beach. Steve felt like a criminal when he was around either of them. He knew it was all his fault. He wished they would just forget the whole thing, but there didn't seem to be much chance of that. There were a few times when he came within a word or two of confessing to John. But he always backed off when he remembered the names they had called each other and thought of how *both* his friends would be mad at him.

"I can't believe it," he thought. "All I wanted was to have a little fun. That lie was supposed to fix up the trouble, not make it worse."

He went out into the kitchen. His mother and father were both kneeling on the cracked tile floor by the sink. Dad had his head poked under the sink and Mom held a rusty wrench and a rag.

"I've got to do something about this problem of mine," Steve said. "It would sure help if you could talk me into it."

Dad's head reappeared and he sat cross-legged on the floor. "That shouldn't be too hard to do as long as you want to be talked into it."

Steve told them his story. "We've got to figure out how you got into this mess," said Mom.

"I've been thinking it was just bad luck," said Steve. "That little lie came out so fast I didn't even think about it."

"Isn't that true of most habits?" asked Dad. "You do things you don't mean to without thinking about them."

"Do you think my lying has become a bad habit?" asked Steve. "I admit I tell some small fibs now and then, but it's usually something very small. Most of the time no one knows about the lie and it doesn't hurt anyone."

"Even harmless lies can start forming the habit," said Mom. "When you start thinking that lying is sometimes a good choice, it makes it easier to do."

"Do you mean we should always tell the truth even if it hurts someone's feelings?" asked Steve.

"Like when they ask you if you like something they did and you really don't?"

"Hmmm," said Dad. "That's different. I'm not sure how to explain it though."

"We don't want to be cruel. Did you lie to John to protect his feelings?" asked Mother.

"No," answered Steve. "It just seemed the easiest way out of a bad situation."

"It certainly seemed like it at the time, didn't it?" said Dad. "I think I know the feeling. Your mom used to ask me to fix something around the apartment, and I usually said I would. Then I forgot about it. If she asked me about it later, and I was feeling guilty about not having fixed it, I would even tell her I had already done it. I guess it seemed like the easiest way to get out of a situation I didn't like. But the few minutes of rest I gained by lying weren't worth the price."

"The price of lying often ends up being steeper than it seems at first," agreed Mom. "The trust of someone you care about is an awful lot to give up. It takes so long to build up trust. Yet we seem to willingly risk it when we lie, just to buy time."

"Sort of like a 'buy now, pay later' deal," said Steve. "Only it's something we can't afford."

"Right," said Dad. "We can't afford to give up a happy marriage or a close friendship. You know, Mom and I were able to build up something good out of that old sore spot about repairs. Now we usually fix things together. That way we help each other get it done and don't make excuses."

Steve peeked under the sink to examine their

31

work on the leaky pipe. "Very professional job," he smiled.

"That's the only type of untruth I'll accept," laughed Dad.

Steve straightened up to leave as his parents clanged their tools back in the toolbox. "It *is* pretty easy to lie," he said. "But I'm not sure I can afford it. Guess I better take care of the bills I already owe."

Steve finally got his friends together by the old lifeguard tower. The white paint was peeling off the tower in ragged scrolls where they leaned against it. John and Brad were uncomfortable and mostly watched their own feet as they dug toes into the warm sand.

"I know you're both going to think I'm a creep," said Steve, "but I was the one that dunked you, John."

Brad and John stared at Steve in disbelief.

It was Steve's turn to stare at his toes. "When I saw how mad you were, John, I thought I could get out of it. I really didn't feel like getting into an argument. Then when you suspected Brad, well, I didn't know how to patch things up."

"You really made me look like a fool," said John, as Steve slowly backed away. "Brad, from now on I wouldn't trust Steve if he signed a confession in blood."

"I'm sorry," said Steve. "Give me another chance."

"I'll tell you what he really needs, John," said Brad. "A good dunking."

"Good idea," said John. "Here I was making such a big deal out of nothing."

As Steve's friends dragged him towards the water,

Steve put up enough of a struggle to make it a challenge for them. "One splash in the water," he thought. "All things considered, that price would be a bargain."

> Therefore, putting away falsehood, let every one speak the truth with his neighbor, for we are members one of another.
>
> Ephesians 4:25

I can't afford to lie, Lord. I don't want to give up one of the best tools you've given us for getting along with others — trust. Help me to understand how valuable trust is.

The Star Who Couldn't Shoot Straight

Todd's eyes followed the white volleyball floating over his head. As the ball came down to one of his teammates in the back row, Todd inched closer to the net. He bent his knees slightly, waiting to leap and tap the ball over the net when it came to him. But the back row player hit the ball poorly, and it headed for Todd's feet. Todd dropped to his knees and tried to scoop the ball over the net. But it got caught in the net and dropped to the floor.

"That's the winning point!" yelled the other team captain as his teammates left the court, whooping and clapping. Todd swung his arm in frustration.

"You gave it a nice try, Todd," said his friend Billy.

"Aw, someone like Aaron or Dan could have gotten it over the net," he said. The two walked wearily through the gym door.

"Think how I feel," offered Billy. "Just when we

could have won the game, I hit my serve out of bounds. I still can't believe it." Todd had been pretty upset himself when Billy had missed that serve.

"Sometimes I think I'd give anything to be really good at sports," said Todd.

"Me too. It doesn't matter how hard I try, I usually end up losing. Makes me feel like a klutz."

Todd slurped a short drink from the water fountain. "My brother Joe has a high school game tonight. Want to watch?"

"Yeah, I guess so. See you there."

Todd could feel the gymnasium floor shaking even before they walked in. "B-E-A-T! Beat the Rockets!" A band that seemed to be made up of mostly trumpets blared out the school fight song. The home team side of the basketball court nearly overflowed with people stomping in time with the music.

Billy had to shout next to Todd's ear to make himself heard. "There's a spot way up in the corner," he said. Both of them liked to sit high up so they would not be in the way of the bigger high school students. From their high perch they watched Joe drill four long practice shots right through the net.

"Doesn't he ever miss?" exclaimed Billy.

"Wouldn't it be fun to be able to shoot like that?" asked Todd sadly. When the game started, the noise in the gym got even worse. A small cluster of people, mostly parents it seemed, stood up on the visitors' side and cheered their team on. But they were drowned out by the howling and stomping on the home team side whenever the home team scored. Billy still grumbled about how he wished he could shoot a basketball like Joe could. But Todd was getting too nervous to notice him. Whenever it looked like Joe's game would be a close one, Todd started gripping the bleacher seats with both hands.

They could barely hear the whistle blow, but they could see the referee in the striped top and black pants and shoes hold up his arm. Play stopped and the referee pointed at Joe. "That wasn't a foul!" protested Todd, jumping to his feet. "Joe didn't even touch him!"

Todd wasn't the only angry spectator. Most of the high schoolers were booing and a few threw paper cups on the court. Billy was surprised to hear adults as well as students calling the referee names. Todd sat back. "That'll show that fat ref. Maybe he'll keep his eyes open and watch what he's doing."

At halftime Billy and Todd scooted down the aisle to beat the crowd to the popcorn stand. But by the time they got there rows of green and gold letter jackets already surrounded the stand. After buying their popcorn, the two had to scramble to get back to their seats before the second half started.

"We should be more than two points ahead of a team like the Rockets," worried Todd. He absentmindedly gulped fistfuls of popcorn as he watched. Billy's eyes wandered over to the band section. Some of the members were trying to wolf down popcorn before they started in on the next song. The baritone always reminded Billy of a large snake coiled around its victim. It was kind of funny how the band director could watch the game and still direct the band with his left hand. Billy knew that Todd would get mad if he talked about the band while the game was

going on. Though he was starting to lose interest in the game, he settled back to watch again for a while.

"I'd sure hate to be number 14 on our team," he said after a Rocket score.

"I wouldn't mind trading places with him," answered Todd impatiently.

"What for? The man he's guarding has scored quite a few points. And that number 14 hasn't even tried to shoot all game!"

Todd shook his head. "You don't know much about basketball. That guy's name is Tony. Joe tells me about him. Just watch him play on defense."

The Rockets were dribbling the ball downcourt again. Tony held his arms high and stared straight at the Rocket player's midsection. His opponent tried to move left, then spun around and dribbled to the right, but Tony blocked his way both times. Finally the Rocket player jumped and tossed an awkward shot at the basket. The ball hit the rim and bounced off.

"See that? Tony made him take a bad shot," said Todd. "That Rocket player has missed more shots than he's made."

"Tony never shoots, though," said Billy. He peeked down into the bottom of the popcorn container to see if there were enough crumbs left to bother with. He was tired of Todd knowing more about sports.

Tony shuffled back and forth by the side of the basket when his team had the ball. He caught a pass and tossed it back without even bouncing it once. When a time-out was called, Todd turned to look at Billy for the first time since the half started.

"It's not Tony's job to score. Joe says that Tony is the best defensive player on the team. That's his main job. There *was* a time last year when Tony decided he wanted to be a scoring star too. He started shooting the ball even when he was far away from the basket. Sure, he could make some of them. But there were others on the team that could shoot better. After awhile the coach made Tony sit on the bench. You know why?" he laughed. "Tony got so worried about being a star scorer that he forgot about playing defense."

"Wow!" said Billy. "You'd think it would be enough to do well at one thing without trying to hog the whole show." The game resumed and the home team began to stretch their lead. Joe made a couple of jump shots, and even Tony scored on a short rebound basket. But Billy had forgotten about the game. He was deep in thought as he crumpled the paper carton.

"I guess it really isn't so strange that Tony would try too hard to be a scoring star," he said. "A lot of us are doing the same thing."

"What do you mean?" asked Todd.

"You and I have been grumbling about not being super athletes. Maybe we spent so much time worrying about sports that we forget about the things we really are good at."

"You mean things like music or school or building things?" asked Todd.

"Sure. Or even something like being a good friend, or making others feel better when they're sick. We aren't all superstars. Like that part in the Bible about parts of the body. If every part does the same thing, it's not much of a body." Billy ended that last statement with a frown. "Now I wonder if I should even bother to play sports."

"Sure you should!" smiled Todd. "Even Tony likes to shoot baskets in practice. We can enjoy sports and try our best. Just so we're careful that being a star isn't the most important thing in our lives."

"You know what made me think about all this?" said Billy. "That foul they called on your brother."

"What about it?" Todd was still angry at the referee.

"Everyone here seemed so worried about winning they forgot everything else they ever learned. You should have seen yourself! And some of the things the crowd yelled at the referee. I'll bet most of the fans are really very good at treating people decently. But we're so busy making sure our team is the star, we pay no attention to how we act."

Todd felt a little embarrassed. "Yeah, I guess we let sports get in the way of more important jobs. It seems we do more arguing during sports games than when we aren't playing. The first thing we should worry about is doing our jobs as persons." The home team had coasted far ahead as the game drew near the end. Now Tony's teammates were giving him the ball to shoot.

"Tony's done his important job," smiled Todd. "Now they're going to give him a chance to score." Tony missed three shots, the last one falling short of the rim and barely touching the net. But he was smiling as broadly as any of his teammates when the buzzer sounded to end the game.

40

Physical exercise has some value, but spiritual exercise is valuable in every way, because it promises life both for the present and for the future.

1 Timothy 4:8 TEV

The talents you have given us are valuable gifts, Lord. Thank you. Forgive me when I tell you that those gifts are not enough. Most of all, help me to remember that the gifts are not as important to me as the One who gave them.

What Have They Got
That I Haven't Got?

"I just have to get my gloves on, Bryan. You can go on ahead to the garage."

Bryan stepped over the crusted snow to the side door. As he walked in he could not get over how clean Wayne's garage was. Why, there didn't even seem to be any oil spots at all on the cement floor! All the tools were hung up on spike-length nails sticking out of pegboard. It wasn't at all like the garage at home with old crates and boxes piled in a heap and greasy tools lying around everywhere.

"Wow!" Bryan said aloud as he saw the bicycle standing next to a well-lit work bench. So that was the big Christmas present that Wayne had been hinting about. The bike was bright blue with red and gold stripes and polished chrome. Even the seat was a shiny royal blue.

"I see you found my present," said Wayne, clos-

ing the door behind him. "What do you think of it?"

"Great!" said Bryan, moving closer to the bike. He suddenly noticed the gears and the series of sprockets by the back wheel. "A 10-speed!" Bryan's eyes nearly bugged out. "Man, how am I going to keep up with you now?"

Wayne grinned proudly. "Try lifting it once."

Bryan grasped the frame and lifted. It was so light it was like carrying a lawn chair. Bryan shook his head in amazement.

"Do you want to try it out?" offered Wayne.

"You're kidding! In the middle of winter?" asked Bryan.

"It's all right. The roads are clear, and you're dressed warm enough. I already broke it in most of yesterday afternoon. Go ahead and take a few spins around the block.

"Thanks," said Bryan as he climbed on. It felt awkward to be leaning so far forward on a bike. He coasted nervously down the slight incline of the driveway. The gears switched so smoothly they did not even make a noise. Bryan gained speed pedaling down a long straightaway and felt like he was zooming. "I hardly had to work at it to get up that speed," he thought. "And to think, I still wasn't even in high gear!"

"You sure are lucky to get a present like that," said Bryan, returning red-faced from the cold wind.

"That's nothing," shrugged Wayne. "You should see the tape deck that Wesley Adams got from his folks. I'll bet it cost twice as much as my bike. What did you get, anyway?" he asked, as he carefully walked his bike back into the garage.

Bryan felt a little embarrassed. "Nothing like this, that's for sure. Mom gave me a sweater and Dad got me a desk lamp. Ken gave me some model paints and, let's see, I guess I got a book from my sister."

Walking home, Bryan could not help feeling a bit envious. When he compared with all his friends, it seemed they always got more than he did. Why couldn't he get something like a bike just once?

"I know, I know," he said to himself. "It doesn't matter what other people do. Maybe my parents can't afford it or maybe there's some other reason." He thought back to Christmas Eve when his family was opening presents. He had really been quite pleased with his gifts, especially the paints and the lamp. It was not until he heard what others were getting that he was disappointed. "I guess my presents are just as good as theirs," he finally decided. "And even if they aren't, so what? I'd rather have my parents than anyone else's, even if they don't give expensive gifts."

It felt good to duck in the back door and get out of the wind. Bryan could not see much with his glasses all fogged up, but he could hear his mother talking on the phone. He took off his glasses and squinted into the closet to find a hanger for his coat. He shivered slightly and walked over to a heat register to warm up. Bryan could tell that his mother was talking to one of her friends. Normally he wasn't too interested in his mom's phone conversations, but as he listened he overheard something that made him forget about how cold he was.

"Oh, I know," his mother was saying. "The Pearson family must be the luckiest people on earth. Their house is just out of this world! I was in there last week, and I swear you could get lost, there are that many rooms. The carpet is so thick you can hardly see your feet! Oh," she sighed, "sometimes I think I'd give anything to trade places with Arlene Pearson."

"Pearsons," thought Bryan bitterly. "Tracy Pearson is a grade ahead of me. The guy is nothing but a troublemaker. He's always making fun of his parents. Ken even tells me that Tracy talks back to them and does whatever he feels like no matter what they tell him. And Mom wants to trade places with Mrs. Pearson. Sure, she would trade me for Tracy as long as she could have that house."

The more he listened, the angrier he got. "What about me?" he thought. "I have to settle for cruddy old paints and stuff when everyone else gets bikes and tape decks. All I have to do, though, is open my mouth about it and I get this big speech about how none of that is important. To think I almost believed it!"

That night Bryan seemed to have lost all his energy. His mother noticed that he kept to himself and didn't say much, but she remembered that was the way he was when Christmas break was almost over.

The next night Bryan's brother Ken ran down the stairs and nearly tripped over a pile of presents halfway up the stairway. He saw that the clear plastic package had not even been broken on the paint set, and the cord was still wrapped tightly around the base of the lamp.

"Hey, Bryan," Ken called. "Are you ever going to use that lamp Dad gave you? You could make a great working area for your models if you put it down-stairs next to the tool bench."

"I suppose I could find a spot for it," said Bryan.

"What's wrong with you?" asked Ken. "You act like you don't even care about your presents. I thought you liked them."

"Oh, they're nice. Nothing like a 10-speed bike though," he tried to mumble, but other ears caught the remark.

"What's this about a 10-speed?" asked Dad, who suddenly appeared in the hallway. Bryan could see his mom had put her book down in the living room and was watching them through the doorway.

"Wayne got a new bike for Christmas. It doesn't seem fair that I never get anything like that."

"We've been over that many times," said Dad. "There are more important things than how much you spend on a present. We should just be thankful for . . . "

"I hear that a lot," complained Bryan. "But no one seems to believe it."

"What do you mean?" asked Mom, coming over to join them.

Bryan felt embarrassed. He didn't like to argue with his parents and wished he had never brought up the subject. "I was really happy with Christmas, even after I tried out Wayne's bike. I tried to remember that I'm luckier than most kids because you give me more than just presents. Then I heard how Mom wishes she could trade places with Mrs. Pearson just because of her big house with the great carpet. But her kids don't think nearly as much of her as I do of

47

you. It makes me wonder what really *is* more important."

Mom bit her lip. "I guess I did say that on the phone, didn't I? Talk about saying one thing and doing the opposite. I'm afraid I haven't been a very good parent."

"You're not the only one guilty of it," confessed Dad. "I've probably said many times that I wished I could have a new car like the Pearsons instead of the rusty station wagon. And remember when Herb got that automatic garage opener? As soon as I saw it I had to rush out and buy one too. I didn't even look to see if there was a way we could have used the money better."

"I just got to thinking that nobody else believes that talk about expensive presents not being important. It seemed I had a right to be mad about the bike," said Bryan.

"I think it's natural to sometimes want what others have," said Ken. "We figure we deserve it as much as they do."

"We forget what is important," said Dad, "but Jesus didn't. Remember when the devil offered him all the riches of the world? Jesus said those things did not rate very high on the list of things he wanted in the world."

"You know, a trade with the Pearsons or anyone else wouldn't make me any happier than I am now," said Mom. "You're right, Bryan, my family is one thing too valuable to give up. We really should remember to be grateful for what we have."

"You helped us remember an important lesson," said Dad. "We can't be happy wishing for things that

48

others have. We'll be happier making sure that each of us gets plenty of love and attention."

"Yeah, I guess that's a lot more important," smiled Bryan.

> Watch out and guard your-
> selves from every kind of greed;
> because a person's true life is
> not made up of the things he
> owns, no matter how rich he may
> be.
>
> Luke 12:15 TEV

We've heard it so often, Lord, that there is much more to life than money and luxuries. It's easy to say that, but it's hard to always live as though we mean it. Don't let greed drive us away from the enjoyment of the gifts you have already given us.

I Don't Understand

It was an awkward silence. No one felt more embarrassed than Jim, who had been the one who asked the question. "Why should we believe all this stuff about God and Jesus?" The question had been gnawing at him for some time, and he had meant it very seriously. He had heard friends, even people he thought were Christians, doubting that it was all true.

Unfortunately, several people in the class laughed when he posed the question. Jim had been a trouble-maker often enough in class for the others to think he was at it again. It had taken all the guts Jim had to raise his hand, but now he backed off. He smiled as if it were all a joke.

Pastor Johnson was not amused. "Are you trying to entertain us, or are you asking a serious question?"

Jim slumped a little lower in his chair. "I'm sorry,

Pastor Johnson," he said. Some of his classmates were still trying to hold back their chuckles. Pastor Johnson continued with the lesson, but he seemed to have lost his concentration. He was no longer his cheerful self, and he lost his place several times during the lesson. Jim noticed several of the minister's stern glances directed at him.

"Let's end tonight with a prayer," said the pastor. It was a good 10 minutes earlier than the usual dismissal. Jim felt bad for having spoiled the lesson. When the prayer was over, he tried to avoid his friends.

"You go on ahead," Jim winked at them. "I've got to clear things up with the pastor." When the room was nearly empty, he approached Pastor Johnson. "Do you have a few minutes?" he asked.

"That depends," the minister answered wearily.

"I'm sorry about what happened in class, but I honestly didn't mean it as a joke."

Pastor Johnson looked hard at the boy, but Jim would not return his stare. "I guess I'm the one who should apologize," said the pastor. "I very nearly let an important moment get away from me. Would you like to come into my study?"

Jim had never seen so many books in one room other than at a library. Except for a few psychology books, they all had to do with the Bible. Instead of taking the chair behind his desk, Pastor Johnson sat in a small, straight-backed chair next to Jim.

"Sometimes it's easier to talk one-to-one, isn't it? How did you put your question?" he asked.

It still felt awkward to ask it. "How come, or why should we believe all this about God and Jesus?" he

51

asked. "A lot of people I'm around say it's all crazy. Some of them are even people who go to church. I'm having a hard time knowing what to think anymore."

Pastor Johnson nodded and pressed his fingers together. "Let me start out this way. What makes you or your friends doubt that what we say about God or Jesus is true?"

"It seems like such a faraway tale sometimes. You know we read about people believing in rain gods and love goddesses long ago. Well, now we think of that as superstition. What about *our* religion? A hundred years from now are people going to think we were all superstitious? I guess I'm looking for some kind of proof."

"You seem to have thought about this a good deal, Jim. Can you prove that God does not exist?"

Jim looked out the window at the newly cut church lawn. "No, I can't."

"That's the trouble with what we call proof in this case. Not everything can be proved or disproved. There are many things that can only be believed."

"It seems to me that everything but religion can be proved, especially with science as advanced as it is. That's what makes me wonder about religion."

"Do you mind if I have a cup of coffee? My wife tells me I can't think without it," smiled Pastor Johnson. "I *believe* that I know which candidate to vote for in the election next week. But I have no way of being absolutely certain I'm choosing the right person. There I'm going on faith. I also remember from my chemistry that there are several views concerning the structure of matter and atoms. Even scientists operate on faith."

"But sometimes when I pray, I wonder if I'm really talking to anyone." Jim sat stiffly in his chair. Talking to a pastor was a new experience for him.

"I admit there is a risk involved," answered the pastor. "What *if* you are just talking to yourself when you pray? Would it be easier for you if there were no risk to it?"

"Yeah, I guess so."

"What would you have to do in order to remove the risk that you might not be really talking to God?"

"I don't know. I guess I'd have to know an awful lot more than I do now. The only way you can be certain of everything is to know everything." Jim laughed nervously. "And if you knew everything, you would be God."

"You've made the key point right there," said Pastor Johnson, taking a sip from his cup. "There are a good many things that only God can know. If we ask him for proof, we are really asking that he make gods out of us."

Jim edged out of his chair as if to leave. "I've felt like a creep for asking myself all these questions the last few months. At least now I know why I felt bad. I don't ask for much do I? I want to know as much as God does, and if I can't then I doubt he even exists."

"Hold on there," said the pastor. "I'm afraid I can't let you leave on that note. I don't think God considers you a creep for asking your questions. In fact, I'll bet he's quite pleased."

"Why would he be pleased that I questioned

53

whether he was real? I would think that's the worst thing you could do."

"A far worse thing to do is to ignore him, Jim. You certainly have not been doing that. You have obviously spent many hours trying to find out about God and that shows how interested you are in him."

Jim rested back into his chair for the first time. "That makes me feel better. I thought I was some kind of criminal."

"You forget that, as much as you want to be with God, he wants you even more. When you start wandering astray, he works hard to get you back. You don't have to feel that it's all up to you to find God. All I ask is that you do not disbelieve just because you cannot understand everything. If everyone did that, this church wouldn't be here."

Again Jim rose to leave, but he kept his hand on the arm of the chair. "I hope you don't mind if I ask you one more question?"

"After tonight I don't think I'll ever fear your questions quite so much again," he answered.

"Well, some of my friends and parents' friends that are what you might call strong churchgoers seem to say it's not so important to believe in Jesus. What's really important is that we act toward people with love. They say the main thing is to live right."

"I've heard that kind of talk too," nodded Pastor Johnson. "Your father is a carpenter, isn't he? If you wanted to be a carpenter, how would you go about it?"

Jim held his chin in his hand. "I'd probably get some tools and ask my dad or someone to teach me."

"You wouldn't just go out and start?"

"Can you imagine the mess I'd make if I did?"

Pastor Johnson spread his arms helplessly. "Why is it any different for a Christian? If people are interested in leading right lives, what makes them think it will just come naturally to them? I would think it would be very hard to live right without an expert to help you. Jesus is the expert; why not take advantage of him?"

"It reminds me of the explorers looking for the source of the Mississippi River. Many of them claimed to have found it, but they didn't look far enough. It took a long time before they found where the river really began."

"You mean that talking about a right life without Christ is like saying that a river can start in midstream?" asked Jim.

"Almost. You don't have to know where a river starts to enjoy it, but that doesn't change the fact that it starts at its source. If you want to know where love starts, make sure you look far enough."

Jim stood up for a third time, but this time he was ready to leave. "Thanks for your time, pastor."

"Thank you for yours."

> I do have faith, but not enough.
> Help me have more!
>
> Mark 9:24 TEV

Dear God, you have given us curious minds to help us learn about you and your world. We would love to be able to figure you out, though we know it isn't possible. Keep us from becoming so frustrated that we give up our search to know you.

Neither Rain Nor Sleet

Saturday was usually a busy day for Darrel. He was often so involved in running around with his friends that he rarely saw the rest of the family except at mealtimes. But today the action was slow. Everyone he knew either had to go to a wedding or visit relatives out of town. He sat in the large living room armchair staring out the window at the icicles dripping in the sunlight.

"There must be something to do," Darrel thought. But the longer he lounged in the chair, the lazier he felt. Suddenly he heard his mother's footsteps coming down the stairs. He scrambled to his feet and searched for something to help him look busy. Mom had a way of finding things for idle hands to do. It always seemed to involve cleaning, especially on a Saturday. Darrel remembered the overstuffed game closet that his parents had been after him to clean up for quite some time.

"Is the mail in yet?" asked Mom, straightening magazines on an end table.

Darrel leaned close to the front window. "Not yet. Mr. Montgomery just got out of his truck, and he's starting on the other side of the street."

Mom walked over to look for herself. "That sure is a heavy-looking mail sack for a Saturday. Poor man, I wonder how much longer he can handle a load like that. He's getting close to retirement, and I hear his back isn't holding up very well."

Darrel eyed his mother's figure. She was dressed in cleaning clothes right down to her frayed tennis shoes. He could hear the scraping and shuffling of his dad doing some work in the basement. His mom's pity for Mr. Montgomery finally gave him an idea. "Why don't I go out and help him today," he said as he reached inside the closet for a jacket.

"Well, that's very thoughtful but . . . " Darrel did not hear the rest; the door was already closing behind him. Mr. Montgomery was probably the slowest mailman in town. He was not much taller than Darrel, and he was very thin. Though the mailman wore a hat on his rounds, Darrel remembered from seeing him in church that he was nearly bald. Even in church he seemed to walk slowly, almost with a limp. Mom was always worrying about Mr. Montgomery. But he had delivered the mail to their house ever since Darrel could remember.

"Hi, Mr. Montgomery. How about if I carried your mail for awhile?"

The little man stopped and laughed. "No, thank

you, young man. Now don't tell me, you're Eleanor's boy, aren't you? Your name is Darrel?"

Darrel nodded proudly. "Really, I'd be glad to help out. At least I could carry it a little ways. It looks pretty heavy."

"No worse than usual," he said, turning up a neighbor's walk.

Darrel stayed right at his heels. "How about if I just keep you company?"

"An excellent offer. I'm afraid you won't find it very exciting, though. Hello, Mr. Weiss," he smiled as the door opened. "Yes, it's warming up. Seems as though spring is finally on the way."

"I'm something like you," said Darrel as they went on to the next house. "I have a paper route."

"Glad to meet one of the kindred," Mr. Montgomery replied. "How long have you been at it now?"

"Almost a year."

"I've delivered mail in this town for 22 years," said the mailman.

"That's a lot of mail. How many letters do you think you've carried in all that time?"

"I have no idea," he said. He pulled out another wad of mail and tucked it in a long black box with a golden eagle emblem on the lid.

Darrel could not remember when he last walked so slowly. "I'll bet you wish you didn't have to carry so much. Wouldn't it be kind of fun if you could walk around with just a couple letters in your bag?"

"Heavens, no!" said Mr. Montgomery. "To tell you the truth, the heavier it is, the better I like it. Watch out for that puddle now."

Darrel easily hopped over the puddle. "I don't

understand why you get such a kick out of carrying a heavy mail bag around all day."

"I warned you it wasn't exciting," he answered. "Darrel, do you like to share with other people?"

"Sure," shrugged Darrel halfheartedly. He was not so sure he *liked* sharing. Sharing usually meant he had to give up something he wanted to someone else, often, it seemed, for no good reason.

"Then you know something of what a good feeling it is," said Mr. Montgomery. "A mailman gets to share all day long. You just watch how many people on this block snatch the mail out of their boxes as soon as I've delivered it. That shows they look forward to it. I can make them happy just by giving them what's in my bag. I don't even have to write the letters. My bag is full when I start out and I spend the whole day sharing it. I say the more I can give, the better."

"Is it really worth the bother? I mean, don't you ever worry about your back?" Darrel could picture his mother fretting about the poor mailman.

"What if I did worry about myself?" said Mr. Montgomery without raising his voice. "Suppose I worried about my back or shoulder and just felt like taking a nice hike. I could deliver as many letters as I felt like and toss the rest away."

"You would have a lot of people mad at you," said Darrel.

"Worse than that, everyone would be confused. They couldn't communicate important messages or hear about people they loved like a niece or a grandson growing up, or an old friend from their hometown. Some might say they would be glad not to see bills, but really even bills are easy ways of letting you pay for what you bought."

"I can see your point," said Darrel. "The whole system would be worthless, but is that any reason to wish for lots to carry?"

The mailman nodded toward the house that they were passing. "Do you know who lives here?" Darrel shook his head. "That is Mrs. Helmes' house. She is in her 80s and lives all alone. Has trouble walking, doesn't get out much. She's a person who could use some mail, but many is the day when I have to walk by because I have nothing for her. Then I would give anything for a little more weight in this bag to carry around for her."

"That's strange," said Darrel. "I sometimes get mad if I have to share and you get upset when you can't."

"Bear one another's burdens, it says in the Bible," said Mr. Montgomery. "We might sometimes think we can save strain on ourselves by not sharing. But I think we would find it would be terrible if we could not share with people."

"Maybe you're right," said Darrel. "It's a good thing God has taken care of that. When you think about it, most of us have more to share than we realize."

"Yes, like the postal service, God gives me plenty to share. We all have time and talent to spread around brightening other people's days. If we don't deliver . . ."

"Then the system falls apart, huh?" interrupted Darrel. "I suppose I should be more like you and wish for more to share than for an easier load."

"God needs mailmen," laughed the little man. "The more of them we have around, the less we each have to carry. That's the end of my route, Darrel. Thank you for 'sharing' your time."

"You really do have a neat job," said Darrel as he started back to his house.

That evening Darrel and his dad joined Mom in the living room.

"All finished," said Dad.

"Thank you for cleaning the game closet, you two. It makes me feel so much better now that the job is done."

"The mail must go through," chuckled Darrel.

"What in the world is that supposed to mean?" asked his Mom. "By the way, did you give Mr. Montgomery a hand with his mail?"

"No, as a matter of fact, I plan to make his load a little heavier to carry. Do you know a lady named Mrs. Helmes?"

"You mean on the end of Lilac Court?" asked Dad. "No, not very well. Why?"

"It's a long story. I'll tell you when I finish writing this letter."

> Give to others, and God will give to you.
>
> Luke 6:38 TEV

Lord, there is plenty for everyone. But it doesn't always get to where it is supposed to go because we stockpile it for ourselves. Help me to share what I can.

Where Friends Are Found

The temperature must have plunged 20 degrees in the last hour. Joel dug his hands into the torn pockets of a jacket that was too flimsy for the unexpected cold. When the most biting gusts of wind swept over him, he scrunched his shoulders together and bent his face low against his chest. Through his watery eyes he could see leaves and pages of old newspapers tumbling across the street.

There was a stoplight on Fourth Street about three blocks from Joel's house. Every corner thereafter was patrolled by stoplights and, occasionally, a policeman. As Joel walked along, the old brick office buildings, the glass-fronted stores and bars, and the skyscrapers all seemed to huddle close together on the street as if they, too, felt the freezing wind.

The nearer Joel drew to the modern department stores, the larger grew the crowds of shivering peo-

ple all around him, especially at street corners. "Thousands of people all around, and I don't even have one friend," thought Joel. This last month, October, had been even worse than the first month of school.

The new school year was supposed to have ended his loneliness. Surely he would find replacements for Carlos and Manuel who had moved away in June. But the school year that had started out so hopefully seemed to be nothing but another series of crowds in which he was alone. Already he thought of the months ahead with gloom. Whenever he saw others in small groups, laughing with friends or even getting caught fooling around in class with their buddies, he felt another step further from anyone his age.

The traffic light changed to green, and Joel surged forward with the crowd. For awhile he wandered aimlessly, pushing through a revolving door into a warm store when he could stand the cold no more.

"It took an awful long time to make friends with Manuel," he thought. His thoughts were interrupted by the sound of laughter. Joel turned to see three young women discussing a bus schedule. Then a well-dressed man in a hurry bumped into him, not even bothering to say excuse me.

Getting tired of people, Joel headed down Tenth Avenue, away from the more popular downtown section. The wind was at his back now and there were fewer people on the street.

Joel could see an old man a block away. The man wore baggy, dark green work pants and a light jacket zipped to the neck. A crutch propped against the store window showed that this man sitting on the sidewalk was crippled in some way. As he drew nearer, Joel saw that one of the trouser legs was empty. The old man's eyes were glazed and his ears and nose bright red. He looked as though he had not shaved in a week.

"Pencils," the man mumbled, and Joel thought he heard something about rent being due. The man's fingers were whitish as they clenched a bundle of new pencils. The tin cup in his other hand must have numbed those fingers even worse.

While Joel stopped to search his pockets for change, a young man with a backpack walked up. His hair blew over his face and his beard was frosted white around the mouth.

"Kind of a cold place to sit, isn't it, mister?" he asked.

"Pencils," said the man, not even looking up.

"Look at your hands!" The bearded man pulled off his backpack in alarm. "Here, we'd better get you inside." The old man was heavy and stiff from the cold. The bearded man nearly fell trying to support his weight. Joel reached over shyly and steadied the old man while the other caught his balance. Then he backed away while the young man put the older man's arms around his shoulder and eased him into the store.

Peeking inside, Joel could only make out that the bearded man was trying to ask the older one some questions. Then the young man picked up a phone book and thumbed through the pages. Joel headed for home.

"It's lucky for that old man that someone came along to help," thought Joel. He felt happy and sad at the same time. He could not help but feel sorry for the old man, but at least it was a welcome sight to see someone do a good deed.

Joel wondered who the bearded man was. "That's the kind of guy I would like to have as a friend," he said. "But then a guy like that probably doesn't need any friends. He could make them wherever he went." The whole thing seemed unfair to Joel. Why was it that the people you wanted as friends were the ones you couldn't get as friends?

Joel passed an old white church with a large message board outside it. This was the first time he could remember there not being some clever saying on the board. He remembered one of them in particular: "Need a friend? Be a friend!"

"Those guys back there had it all backwards," he smiled. "The bearded man was *being* a friend even though it was the old man who *needed* a friend. The bearded man wasn't likely to get anything from the old man, yet he helped him anyway."

"Maybe that's what the message board meant," he thought suddenly. "Maybe my trouble is that I'm wanting only friends that already have friends, friends who will do *me* some good. Just a few minutes ago it was the bearded guy I wanted for a friend when it was the older one who needed a friend. I suppose you can't expect to find friends when you don't act like one. Really, I'll bet it's easy to find friends. But everyone is so busy wanting only certain friends they forget about being a friend."

Joel was glad the wind was behind him as he walked along toward home. The cold wind on his forehead had been giving him a headache. He glanced back one more time and saw the backpack and the crutch still outside the entrance to the store.

By the next weekend the cold snap had broken. "Wouldn't you know it, now I'm wearing a jacket that's too heavy," thought Joel. He could hear the faint ringing as he held the phone to his ear.

"Hello?"

"Hi, Mom. It's Joel. I'm over at a house on Eighth Street across from the park."

"Really!" she exclaimed. "On such a nice day I would have thought you would be outside. There won't be many more of these days this year."

"I know. We're going outside in a minute. There's a guy here that I met last week who's never ridden a city bus before. His name is Ryan. I told him it was simple to do but he could go with me once and I could show him all the tricks. Just thought I should let you know so you aren't wondering where I am."

"Thanks. It sounds fine to me. It's good to know you are finding some friends."

"Yeah," he grinned at Ryan. "It took me awhile to find out where they all were hiding. Well, I'll be back by suppertime. Bye!"

> If you do good to those who do good to you, what credit is that to you? For even sinners do the same.
>
> Luke 6:33

You've heard me ask for friends, Lord. Is it friends that I want or popularity? Help me to make the first move to be a friend.

68

Just for Emergencies

Eleven-fifteen. Bruce could not ever remember a morning passing as slowly as this one was. His eyes had already searched out everything there was to see in that hospital room. He had seen every dial on the wall, every tile on the ceiling, every flower on the window ledge, and every bolt on the bed frame. No matter how many times he saw them, they looked cold and strange. The television was just as unsettling, full of dull shows whose titles he had never heard of.

Eleven-nineteen. Mom would be in at one o'clock. A few more tests would come later on, and then the surgery would be tomorrow morning. Bruce wondered what kind of knife they used. Every time he thought of that knife going into his back and playing with his spine, he broke into a cold sweat. He was glad his roommate was sleeping because he did not feel like talking to a stranger.

Eleven–twenty-one. He tried to lay back and adjust the bed to a more comfortable setting, but his muscles were so tense that a few seconds in any position resulted in a dull ache. "No one else in my family has ever been in the hospital for an operation," he thought. "How come the clock only says 11:24?"

Knock, knock. Bruce twisted slowly under the covers to see what the nurses wanted this time. Expecting to see all-white uniforms, he was startled by the contrasting gray suit. "Good morning, Bruce," said Pastor Jefferson.

It was the older assistant pastor at church. Everyone called him Pastor Jeff. Bruce loved his deep, droning voice when he preached. Pastor Jeff rarely smiled with his mouth, yet he was friendly. He always had time for kids, and he never failed to get one of his stories in when he visited a Sunday school class.

"Hi," said Bruce. "Am I ever glad to see you!"

"It's a good day in which to be glad. After all it is a day that the Lord has made." Bruce smiled in spite of his operation worries. Pastor Jeff always had a Bible verse handy. He must have the whole Bible memorized.

"I'm afraid I don't feel glad about much today," said Bruce. He sank back into his bed as he remembered why Pastor Jeff was visiting him. The pastor pulled a chair close to the bed, sat down, and put a hand on Bruce's shoulder.

"I'm sure there are many easier things to do than go through an operation like this," he said.

70

"Pastor, I'm going to scream if this day doesn't start to go faster. I wish they would knock me out and be done with it. Then I think of how it will be when I wake up. I know it will hurt. The thought of being cut up is driving me crazy."

"Bruce, do you know why the Lord sends pastors and friends to people like you at times like this?"

"Sure," sighed Bruce. "You're supposed to try and cheer me up and help me face up to the operation. God sure asks a lot of you, doesn't he?"

"He asks very little of me. He's the one who does the cheering. Have I ever told you the story of the shipbuilder?" asked Pastor Jeff.

Bruce shook his head. Pastor Jeff went on in a powerful monotone, almost like a chant, and Bruce felt a little better just listening to him talk. He hoped for a long story so the voice would not stop.

"A long time ago a shipbuilder was working on a large boat for his son. He spent several years getting every detail right. When it was finally ready, the son thanked him and prepared to set sail across the sea. Some of the crew told him it would be smart to give it a short trial run before going out onto the high seas with it.

" 'We don't want to wait until we're too far from shore before we find out if it will sail well,' they told him.

"But the shipbuilder's son refused, and they headed out onto the sea. When the waves began to swell beneath the boat, the crew asked him if he was anxious about his untested ship. The son answered, 'My father built this boat for me. He knew that I would face storms. He has seen to it that everything

71

is built as well as it could be, so I am not worried about the ship.'

"Bruce, you know who made the world you're living in. You know who made you and the surgeon. Your Father knows the storms you may face in life. He wouldn't let you face them unprepared. Remembering who is in charge may help ease your fears."

"I know, Pastor Jeff. I know I shouldn't worry. But it still bothers me. When I imagine the knife, I know that God is really in control, but I can't help feeling this way. I get so nervous my whole body shakes. I'm afraid, and I can't sleep or forget about this operation even for one minute."

Pastor Jeff leaned closer to Bruce. "Bruce, I hope you never get tired of stories, as long as they are good ones. I want to tell you about something that's happened in my life. When I was younger, I was fortunate to be able to go to college. It wasn't easy for me because there were many brighter students at the school. When it came time for my final tests, I was ready to give up and go home. I would get so worried about failing tests that I could not even study. That got me all the more behind and caused me even more worry. I was desperately afraid of failing.

"But just before I had to take those first exams, I received a package from home. It was stuffed full of oranges, cheese, crackers, gumdrops, and my favorite cookies. I think they included some tea, some new pencils, even some aspirin. At the bottom of the package was a cheery note. My parents must have known that it was an extra hard time for me, and they sent me some emergency relief. As I went through

72

school, I always found one of those packages the week before the final tests. And it always helped."

Bruce looked confused. He wondered if that was the end of the story.

"Bruce, God knows when you face an extra challenge. He has prepared an emergency relief package for you. It's something called adrenaline. Adrenaline makes your heart beat faster, rushes blood to your muscles and nerves, and keeps you alert. It makes you feel nervous and uncomfortable because it boosts your body's power level a little higher than usual. Adrenaline always flows when your body thinks you will be needing some extra strength."

"Is that why I'm so nervous about the operation?"

"Partly," said Pastor Jeff. "You can use it to your advantage by letting it remind you that God is with you. You see, God can use even fear to his advantage. He has cooked up this emergency relief for you to help you through the difficult times."

"You mean it's normal to feel this way?" asked Bruce.

"I think so. Do you remember a king named Hezekiah in the Old Testament? He found a huge army camped outside his city, waiting to destroy it. I think he felt the same way. But he never quit believing that God was with him. Can you think of others in the Bible who might have felt this way?"

Bruce needed only a few seconds to think. "Jesus in the Garden of Gethsemane before he was captured." Bruce and Pastor Jeff spoke for a few more minutes until a nurse appeared with a full tray of food for his roommate.

"Lunchtime already?" asked Bruce. Sure enough, the clock read 12:35.

> God is our refuge and strength,
> a very present help in trouble.
> Psalm 46:1

I always need you, Jesus. But there are times when I'm especially afraid. Then I need to feel you close, almost close enough to touch. Thank you for being there when I need you.

Old-Fashioned Parents

"This must be the crookedest creek in the world," said Paul Rose. "If we weren't going so slow we would all be dizzy by now." His twin brother Perry and their friend Rollie hopped across the flat stones in their bare feet. They had spent all afternoon in the creek. Chasing minnows, digging after crayfish, and skipping stones made the time fly by. Occasionally a kingfisher with its "rat-a-tat" call or a muskrat bobbing its head out of the water added to their enjoyment.

"Why don't we each grab a leaf and race it downstream?" suggested Rollie.

"OK," said Perry. "The first one to reach that bridge way downstream wins." Perry's leaf found the shortest path through the stream that tumbled over and around small rapids of stones. But it became wedged against two rocks. Paul's was caught in

a backwater, so Rollie's leaf won easily. The twins demanded a rematch which Perry won.

"This really has been a fun day out here in the sticks," sighed Perry as the three kept splashing downstream. "You're lucky to have all this in your backyard. I'm glad our parents are letting us stay the night."

"Yeah," said Rollie. "I hear your folks are pretty strict."

"Old-fashioned is the word for it," said Paul. "You're practically the only friend we have that they approve of. They think this is still the middle ages and we're still little kids. We can't go to any parties or anything that has dancing. We're not supposed to talk at the supper table. They check all the books we read and the TV shows we watch . . ."

"Wow, my parents aren't nearly that bad," said Rollie.

" . . . Make us save all our money and take piano lessons. Sometimes we have to stay in for not having our room clean enough, if you can imagine!"

"I feel lucky," said Rollie. "I don't get bothered nearly so much."

"You can say that again," said Perry. "Can you imagine if we tried to grow our hair this long!" He lifted up a few of Rollie's curly locks.

"What do you suppose makes your parents like that?" asked Rollie.

"I don't know," said Perry, catching his balance after slipping on a slimy rock. "There doesn't seem to be any way to change their minds. By the way, what time is it getting to be?"

Rollie stared at his watch and held it to his ear.

"Oh, great!" he moaned. "It stopped at exactly ten to six, and who knows how long ago that was!"

"You mean it's *after* six?" asked Paul.

"I'll bet it's closer to seven. Can you believe that? We've been walking down this creek for almost four hours!" said Rollie.

It didn't seem possible that it had been that long since they had wandered into the creek from the ravine behind Rollie's yard. "If we've been gone that long," said Paul, who wasn't quite convinced, "that means it will be dark before we get home."

"Oh, no! We'd better turn around and get going," said Rollie. For awhile none of them spoke as they tried to walk quickly through the water. But the current was stronger than they had thought. That, plus countless toe-stubbings from their haste, made the going much slower than they hoped.

Perry, who had a better sense of direction than the others, saw a path leading up from the left bank of the creek. "Look, that trail leads up in the direction of your house, Rollie. With the way this creek winds all over the place it could save us hours. We'd be home in plenty of time."

The others looked doubtful. "What if it just ends?" asked Rollie. "Or suppose the trail winds around and doesn't end up where you think it will? Then we would really be in trouble when it gets dark."

Paul agreed. "At least there's no way you can get lost following a river."

"You've got to take a chance sometime," argued Perry. But he could not convince the others, and they continued on. The more Perry thought about it, the more certain he was they should have tried the path.

78

He could feel the shadows deepening, and the splashing water was feeling less refreshing and more chilling in the evening air. In the growing blackness they fell more than once on unseen stones. Perry was sure his feet had lost half their skin. After what seemed like hours of getting nowhere, none of them was saying a word.

Perry had been plodding ahead without even watching where he was going. Suddenly something seemed familiar. He stopped and headed back to the left bank.

"Does this tree look familiar to anyone else?" he asked. He heard nothing but sloshing as his companions drew near.

"Sure!" cried Rollie. "That's it! That's the tree we swung from for awhile before we started down the creek. We're back! Look, I've got the rope in my hands."

Paul shuddered. "Do you realize we almost went right past it?" he whispered. "We would have been in the creek all night! Probably would have caught pneumonia."

They scrambled up the steep ravine to Rollie's house. Before they reached it, they knew they were in trouble. Several cars were in the driveway. The kitchen window was all lit up, displaying a roomful of worried people.

Rollie's dad was the only one to greet them with a laugh. When he heard their whole story, he shook his head. "So you were in the creek. You know that path you were talking about leads almost back to the house. We used to take it when I was a boy."

Mr. and Mrs. Rose were there, and they quickly

escorted the twins to the car. "I'm afraid you can't stay overnight. You've caused enough trouble as it is," said Mrs. Rose over her shoulder.

Perry and Paul stared straight ahead from the back seat. Their parents' action had taken the chills out of them. In fact, Paul's face was flushed as he spoke. "It's not fair. The one time you finally let us out of the house and you come running after us."

"You didn't handle it well," said Mr. Rose. "We were worried sick about you. Maybe you need an earlier bedtime to straighten you out."

"I hate always being treated like a baby," fumed Paul. "You know how we lost track of the time? We were talking about you!" He told them what they had been discussing with Rollie. His parents did not speak for a few seconds, and he saw his mother sitting tensely well forward in her seat.

"It's not easy to be a perfect parent," sighed Dad, his eyes never leaving the road. "We want to bring you up right. It's just that there are so many decisions to make. We have to do the best we can. When the right choice isn't clear to us, we fall back on what our parents did. Can you see a better way?"

"I think I know the problem," said Perry. "I've been thinking about that since we debated whether or not to take the path home tonight. We didn't really know what to do, so we ended up taking what we thought was the safest way, the one we were most sure of."

"You're right," said Mom. "That's how we often decide when we have decisions to make as parents. When the chips are down it seems better to go with what you did before."

"But look what happened to us," protested Paul. "We thought we were taking a safe way, and it was nearly the worst choice of all. Rollie didn't recognize our starting point. It turned out to be different than the way he remembered it."

"If we would have taken the chance on the path and not been so scared, we would have been home on time," said Perry. "Why are you so afraid to take a chance on us?"

"Maybe that's the trouble," admitted Dad. "The old, familiar ways aren't always as we remember them, yet we act as if they were."

"Hasn't there been a lot of trouble in the church over the years because people have been afraid to give up old, familiar ways?" asked Paul. He was excited that they were finally discussing this with their parents. "Weren't the Pharisees sticking to the old road when Jesus came along? They wouldn't take a chance on him."

"Yes, Jesus came in with a lot of new ideas," said Dad. "But don't forget he did a lot of the old too. He observed customs, obeyed the Ten Commandments, and read out of the Old Testament."

"So if the old way isn't always best, and the new way isn't either, how do you decide?" asked Perry.

"I think you understand our problem in being parents. We don't have all the answers."

"Maybe we have been holding on to safe, familiar ways with you boys a little too much," said Dad. "After all, you really are growing up. We can't keep you under our wings all the time. But I hope you have a better idea now of why we act the way we do. It's not just to be mean."

Mom turned in her seat. "We may always have a hard time breaking away from what you think are old-fashioned ways. But maybe if we all work at it, we can try to see each other's point of view and maybe we can balance each other out."

"Sure," said Paul. "I think you'll find we're reasonable people."

"Hey, where are you going now?" asked Perry as the car turned into a driveway and backed out.

"If we hurry we can get back before Rollie is in bed," said Dad. "Maybe it's time we took a chance."

> Honor your father and mother.
> . . . Fathers, do not provoke your children to anger.
>
> Ephesians 6:2, 4

Thank you, Jesus, for parents. Life isn't meant to be a tug-of-war between us, is it? I don't always want us to be on different sides. Help us to talk with each other, not at each other.

Girls

"Shh! Adam is a light sleeper," warned Tom. Five other boys in the darkness behind him stopped whispering until they walked a good ways down the path from their counselor's tent. This was just going to be a quick trip, so they all still had their pajamas on. When they broke out of the woods onto a moon-lit trail, they could see how ridiculous they looked, especially with their shoes on. But they did not care because they did not intend to be seen.

Tom stopped just in front of a small clearing. The rest gathered around him and looked into the clearing. Four tents stood in a ring around the clearing. Tom pointed to the two picnic tables and the fire pit filled with wet, gray soot and ash.

"Watch out for those, now," he said. The band split into two groups and circled the tents closest to the path. Quickly they untied the tent stakes and ropes. Chuck could not help laughing out loud as the tents collapsed. The sudden commotion inside the tents sent the boys scurrying back to the trail, pushing and stumbling in their haste. The raid had been a success.

For most of the next day, the raiders gloated over their night's work, especially when Adam was not around. Tom felt braver as the day wore on, and he even started teasing their counselor.

"Did you sleep well last night?" he asked Adam innocently.

The lunch menu called for hot dogs over an open fire. That meant eating at the girls' camp where there was a fire pit. Tom and Chuck ran ahead to the girls' camp. They began teasing the girls, trying to find out who had been in the two tents that fell down.

The meal was a disaster. It seemed like every few seconds an argument broke out. Roger was hooted at for offering to help one of the girls with her hot dog. Chuck flipped his hot dog in the air and tried to catch it, but it fell into the ashes.

"That's enough wasted food," snapped Adam. The boys retreated to a shady clearing and finished their meal. There was no point in pushing their counselor any further.

That night the boys got into a loud fight about who liked which of the girls. "You guys have spent a good deal of excess energy lately," said Adam. "I think we'll skip the campfire tonight and get some extra sleep. I would suggest you get in your tents and stay there." Without another word he walked away, hands on hips.

"All right," sighed Tom, and he crawled off to his

tent. The rest were making moves to do the same when Tom charged back out of his tent. "Who took my sleeping bag?" he challenged.

"No one took your bag," said Chuck. "Here, give me your flashlight." But in a few minutes they discovered that all the bags were gone.

"I know! It must have been the girls in the Far Village. I'll bet they took them to get even for last night!"

"Come on, let's get them back!" The group raced down the trail, shouting threats at the girls. Suddenly the boys leading the pack stopped, and the ones behind them couldn't help running into them. Adam and the girls' counselor, Cheryl, were blocking the way. Even in the shadowy darkness the boys could see that Adam was angry.

"Get that flashlight out of my eyes," he said slowly. "I've found your sleeping bags. If you get back to your tents now you'll have them in a few minutes. Any more trouble and you may have to shiver yourselves to sleep tonight."

The boys turned back, but when they were out of sight Tom yelled, "Don't stay out too late with your girl friend!"

The next morning a warm sun beating down on the tents woke the boys early. But the first ones to crawl out of the tents saw that Adam was already up, standing next to the picnic table. Beside him was a dirty straw hat and a paper bag.

"Morning, Adam. What's the hat for?" said Chuck.

"As soon as everyone gets out here, I'll explain," said Adam loudly. Within five minutes there was a cluster around the picnic table. Adam sat quietly until the last members to arrive laced their shoes.

"Gentlemen, this is first prize in today's contest," he said, pulling a maroon and white shirt out of a bag. The words "Outpost 1" were written across the front.

"Hey, this is going to be good," said Tom.

"The rules of the contest are as follows. Each of you will draw the name of a fellow camper from this hat. For the rest of the day, whenever you are around girls you must act as if you are that person."

"Oh, great! I hope I get Bobby."

"There is one catch," continued Adam. "At suppertime the girls will vote on which of you they liked the best. Step right up." The boys nervously drew names from the hat.

"I got Tom," moaned Chuck. "I'm supposed to act like him and try to get girls to like me?" The rest drew names and Adam wrote down the selections in a book.

"Good luck, gentlemen," he said. Throughout the morning Adam heard mutterings behind him. He also noticed that none of his boys would come within sight of the girls. As they were returning from the swimming hole that morning, Tom finally got up the courage to speak.

"Adam, this is the dumbest game I ever heard of. It's not just me that thinks so. Ask anyone." The rest all nodded.

"You're right," said Adam. "It's one of the dumbest games I've ever heard of. Why don't you all sit around the campfire here, and we'll discuss it." The boys arranged themselves on the huge logs that were lain across notched stumps to form a bench. "Any idea why I suggested this dumb game?"

"It's probably got something to do with our fights with the girls, but I can't figure out what," said Chuck.

"Was it easy acting like someone else?" asked Adam as he calmly whittled on a piece of wood.

"That wouldn't be so hard," said Tom. "But try doing that and getting someone to like you at the same time. That's hard, and dumb." The other boys laughed.

"Tell me," said Adam, looking around the circle of puzzled campers, "have all of you been acting the same around girls as you do otherwise?"

"Are you kidding?" laughed Tom. "Paulson turns into a ladies' man every time he sees a girl."

"Tom's always showing off for them."

"Baker acts like he's Mr. Tough."

"I guess that answers my question," said Adam. "Why do you act that way?"

"You're supposed to be a big man when girls are around," muttered Tom.

"They're different from boys. You don't really know what to do to make them like you," said Chuck.

"I guess some of us try too hard to get them *to* like us and others try too hard *not* to have them like us."

"Do you think you are ready for girl friends?" asked Adam. No one said anything. "I'm not saying you aren't ready. But it's very tough to act like someone you aren't to a friend. It's too much for you or for anyone. As you said, it's a dumb game whether you play by my rules or by your own."

"I suppose girls play the same game," said Tom.

"I'm afraid so," answered Adam.

"No wonder it's been such a mess this week," said Chuck. "Everyone is so busy putting on an act that we can't tell who anyone really is."

"Hey, I vote we give Adam the grand prize!" Tom said, jumping to his feet.

"It was my shirt to begin with," grinned Adam.

"In that case, I vote we split it among ourselves," said Chuck. "Let me borrow your knife."

"Would you settle for a treat at the camp store?" asked Adam. "Good," he concluded as he carefully folded away his shirt.

> When I was a child, I spoke like a child, I thought like a child, I reasoned like a child; when I became a man, I gave up my childish ways.
>
> 1 Corinthians 13:11

Lord, the older I get, the more I hear about girls. I appreciate the difference between boys and girls; but it's hard to know exactly how to act. Help me to know myself, to be the right person around all people.

The Rotten Brother

"From the way Mark is acting you'd think he'd never been to the fair before," thought Keith as he watched his younger brother race around the yard.

"How much time till Matt and Paul get here?" yelled Mark.

Keith glanced at his watch. "About a half hour. Take it easy or you'll be burnt out before we even go. Remember it's nearly a mile walk just to get there."

Mark joined his older brother on the steps and tried to copy his pose. He leaned back lazily on the cement steps with his legs crossed and a long blade of grass between his teeth. But he could not sit still for long, and he ran to find a rubber ball to throw against the steps.

Mark returned in time to see the familiar green metallic bike and blonde hair of Cliff racing toward them. Cliff held a large sheet of paper in one hand and seemed in a desperate hurry. He rode full speed up to the front lawn to where Keith was sitting.

"I'm telling my dad you rode on our lawn!" said Mark fiercely. Neither Cliff nor Keith listened to the scolding. Cliff stayed on his bike, balancing on one foot, and thrust his sheet of paper at Keith.

"Look at this!"

Keith unfolded it and saw a series of short scrawls. They seemed to be signatures of people though he could not make out the names of the first two. Then he saw a clearly written name of a television star and then the autographs of several baseball players.

"Look on the back," puffed Cliff. "I got the governor too!"

Keith looked at his friend suspiciously. "Where did you get these?"

"Let me see!" begged Mark.

Cliff ignored him as he took back his paper. "Down at the golf course. There are so many big name people there I haven't even gotten half of them yet. Grab your bike and a pen and paper and let's go down there before they all leave."

Keith got up to open the door and then stopped. "I'm supposed to wait for Matt. He's bringing his little brother and we're taking Mark to the fair in less than half an hour." Mark grinned at his brother.

"Come on, we'll be back in time," said Cliff impatiently. "Even if we don't, Mark can go with Matt since he's got to take his little brother anyway. And if worse comes to worst, you can go another day. The fair lasts all week. This is a once-in-a-lifetime chance!"

Keith stood holding the door open while he debated what to do. Finally he bent down and put his arm around Mark's shoulder. "Mark, if we don't happen to get back before Matt comes, you can go with him. You won't care if I'm not there as long as you get to go with Paul. Just remember to tell your sister when you leave. I'll try to get back though."

Cliff laughed as they rode down the hill in front of the house. "You know with the lines you'll have to wait in at the golf course, we'll never get back in a half hour."

"Maybe not," said Keith. "But I brought along an extra sheet to get autographs for Matt. When I give him that, he won't be so upset that I didn't come along."

Keith could hear Mark sobbing as he walked his bike into the garage. "What's Mark doing back so soon?" he wondered. "I wasn't gone that long, and he should still be at the fair. Matt couldn't have been this late in picking him up."

But he could tell by the sobs that something had gone wrong. He felt a little guilty about running out on Mark, and he had a suspicion that he was in some trouble.

"Where have you been?" asked both parents at once as Keith stepped in the door. Keith was about to answer when he saw the clock. He had been gone over two hours!

"You were supposed to take Mark to the fair and you just left him here! What were you thinking of!" said Mom. She was holding Mark's head against her shoulder as he sniffled quietly.

"Something came up. I thought Matt would," stumbled Keith. "I'm really sorry, Mark."

"Something came up?" said his dad. "He's not Matt's brother. When Matt got here and found out you had gone off somewhere, he was angry and left without Mark. I don't blame him! But the thing I can't understand is how you could leave a six-year-old boy at home all by himself. Keith, he's too little to take care of himself!"

"Where was Jody?"

"Your sister was baby-sitting down the block. We just got home 10 minutes ago. You've got a lot of explaining to do," said Dad, his voice rising.

Keith lost his temper, and angry words were exchanged before he ended up slamming a door and running upstairs to his room. It didn't take long for his anger to melt away. He knew he was wrong. He was upset that things had turned out this way, but mostly he was upset with himself.

"How in the world could I have done such a mean thing to Mark?" he thought. "He'd been looking forward to it all week. Matt deserved better treatment too. Then I start talking back to my parents and saying things I don't mean. All for a lousy pageful of autographs." He flicked the paper off his desk and watched it flutter to the floor.

Then he sat on the edge of his bed with his knees up to his chin. He began to think of all the things he had done wrong lately. The longer he sat there, the more he remembered. His list seemed to pile until it was way in the hundreds of unkind acts.

"For every sin I remember there are probably 10 more that I managed to forget," he thought. "Why do my parents put up with all this?" Then a worse thought came to him. "Why does God put up with me? I've done too many things for even God to forgive. What if he punishes me?"

He was very near tears, and suddenly he knew what he must do. "I don't deserve another chance," he said out loud. "I don't see how I can talk to my parents or God again. I shouldn't even talk to Mark. He deserves something more than a rotten brother."

Mark peeked around the doorway into Keith's room. He was wearing his cowboy pajamas, and Keith could tell from his shiny, combed hair that was still wet around the edges that he had just come from his bath.

"You're not always a rotten brother," said Mark.

"I am too," Keith said irritably. He listed a couple of weeks worth of bad behavior. "And then I left you alone, and something could have happened to you with no one else around. Besides, you didn't get to the fair like I promised you."

"That's OK," said Mark, walking into the room. "You said you were sorry. You didn't do it to be mean, did you? Can we go to the fair tomorrow?"

"Sure," said Keith. "I don't know why you want me around."

But Mark wasn't paying attention. He looked over Keith's desk and the shelves in the room. "Where are your autlegraphs?"

"That's 'autographs'." Keith almost smiled. "Right here, take a look if you want." He picked up the sheet off the floor and handed it to Mark. "Come on, Mark, you're supposed to go to bed."

As he led Mark into the hall he asked, "You mean

all I have to do is say I'm sorry and you forget the whole thing? Wow! I wish it was that easy with . . . " he paused.

"You wish it were that easy with whom?" asked Dad who was waiting for them by Mark's bed.

Keith stood silently for a few seconds while Mark climbed in bed.

"With you and Mom. And God. It can't be that easy when you've got a list this long to ask forgiveness for." He held his arms out as wide as he could.

Dad gave Mark a hug. "I know you have a wonderful little brother, Keith. But if you think he knows more about forgiveness than God does, you're giving him too much credit. Or you're not giving God enough. Maybe you're not giving Mom and I enough credit either."

"There must come a time when people get tired of forgiving," said Keith. "I think I've used up my chances."

"I wouldn't worry about that," Dad said. "Mark was saying something that God has always said. All you have to do is be sorry for your sins. God knows you're not perfect. He loves us all so much that he's willing to forgive us no matter how many wrong things we do."

"I really am sorry about today, Dad. And Mark."

"You already said that," sighed Mark. "Good night."

"Good night," answered Dad and Keith. As they walked together down the stairs, Dad turned to Keith. "The rest of us have already forgiven you for today. How about forgiving yourself?"

If we confess our sins, he is faithful and just, and will forgive our sins and cleanse us from all unrighteousness.

1 John 1:9

Lord, it's a terrible feeling knowing that I've done something wrong. I've known that feeling more than I care to. But you are able to remove that feeling. Thank you.

Fight! Fight!

"Watch who you're pushing!" came a voice from behind Kirby and with it a shove. Kirby kept his balance and looked back to find the owner of the voice. With the mass of moving bodies in the hall, it took a few seconds before he saw him. A boy in a light blue sweater stood motionless, staring right into Kirby's eyes.

"*You* watch it!" shouted Kirby, shoving the boy back into some onlookers. The boy in the blue sweater slid his books along the floor against the wall, and Kirby handed his books to a friend.

"Fight! Fight!" shouted several kids. At once the helter-skelter movement of the crowd stopped, instead coiling into a tight ring around the two angry boys.

"Great!" muttered Kirby as he saw the crowd grow larger. He was embarrassed by the sudden attention.

It made him even madder at the other boy to think that he was responsible for getting them into this mess. By the way the other boy glanced around like a cornered fox, Kirby could tell that he didn't want an audience either.

Kirby knew only one way to avoid a fight without backing down. "Do that again and you'll be sorry," he said.

"Yeah, we'll see about that." Neither would turn his back on the other while he collected his books again and slipped through the crowd of students. Kirby still felt uncomfortable as he sat on the bus on the way home from school. He had seen plenty of fights at school but so far had been able to steer clear of any himself. This time he had come close.

"What are you supposed to do?" he asked his parents that night as the two played a word game. "Are you supposed to just let people push you around?"

"What was the fight about?" asked Mom, waiting for Dad to complete his move.

"Oh, nothing really. Just a little shoving and it was probably all an accident. But what are you supposed to do when you get pushed into a corner?"

"That's a good question," said Dad. "I was brought up to fight my own battles and stand up to people. But somehow it doesn't seem like a very Christian way of looking at things."

"Yes, it's a tough problem," said Mom. "There was certainly a lot of fighting in the Old Testament. But Jesus didn't fight."

"How about protecting people you love? Or fighting for something you believe in very strongly?" asked Dad.

"You two aren't much help," said Kirby as he left the table to get a drink.

"I'm sorry," Dad said. "But we're all in the same boat. It seems there is a good deal about fighting that we find wrong. Yet we're afraid to say that it's always wrong. I don't like the situation any better than you do."

"Some people say that it's wrong to fight yet it's something you have to do," said Kirby. "That makes even less sense."

"There are some problems we wrestle with our whole lives," said Mom. "Maybe we should all pray about it and ask God to help us find an answer."

A few weeks later Kirby's dad spotted an article in the newspaper about an old crafts festival. The family piled into the car and drove off to see the displays. The crafts festival was held in an open park sectioned off by ropes into smaller areas. Small crowds were clustered around each of the areas.

"Let's try this one first," said Kirby, pointing to a small shack made to look like the open end of a barn. Black smoke billowed out from one side of the barn's entryway, and occasionally a burst of steam rose in a small cloud. A man with forearms that seemed too large for the rest of his body was pounding on a glowing orange rod. A spray of sparks jumped off the rod at every clanging blow from the hammer. With a heavy pair of tongs, the blacksmith placed the metal back in his furnace. Three times he pulled down on a bellows that looked like a giant accordion and watched the flames swell. By the time the blacksmith had hammered the metal into a U-shape, there were drops of sweat running down the sides of his face.

"I almost got tired just watching him," marveled Dad.

"I *am* tired of watching him," said Mom. "I would like to see the glassblowers before they finish their demonstration."

They managed to squeeze their way into a front row position at the side of the glassblowers' exhibit. There they saw a man and woman dressed in colorful clothes almost like circus performers. The man held a long tube with what looked like a small fishbowl at the end of it. He held it as if he were playing a trumpet and twirled it slowly.

The woman attached a smaller piece of glass to the bowl. After several minutes of twirling, twisting, adding pieces, and cutting them off, the two had made a fancy sugar bowl.

"How's that for a demonstration of violence against nonviolence!" asked Kirby.

"What?" said Dad. "Oh, you're still stuck on that fighting problem."

"Yes, we never did answer it. There's something about these two demonstrations that might give a clue."

"Really?" asked Mom. "What were you thinking?"

"Well, the blacksmith was able to shape the metal because of strength. He had to work very hard to make the metal do what he wanted it to. The glassblowers seemed to let gravity do much of the work for them. They let the glass sag towards the ground until it reached the shape they wanted. Then they

100

twisted somehow and let it work itself into another shape."

"And if these craftsmen were dealing with people instead of metal and glass, you would rather be treated like the glass?"

"Yes, that much is obvious," said Kirby. "But I was thinking that, even if I were the craftsmen, I would rather do it the glassblower's way. It sure seems a lot easier than all that pounding. It would be much easier all the way around if we tried to steer things toward the good."

"Well, if the blacksmith could save himself all the effort of that pounding, I'm sure he would," said Mom. "Maybe he proves that there are some times when strength or force is the only thing that will work."

"I would have to want something pretty bad to go to all the work that the blacksmith goes to," said Dad. "I guess it's the same with fighting. Something should be extremely important to us before we consider going to all the work of fighting."

"You really had a good point, Kirby," said Mom. "The blacksmith gets his way by using his *own* power. The glassblower saves himself most of the strain by letting *God's* power, gravity, do the work for him."

"In other words, in fighting we rely on our own power instead of God's?" asked Kirby.

"Yes," said Dad. "Maybe we should always look to God's power first. Then we wouldn't be so quick to get into fights. That means any kind of fighting—hitting, name-calling, you name it."

"Are we getting anywhere with your question on

fighting?" asked Mom. "Or are we still making it worse?"

"It's helped," said Kirby. "At least I know that an accidental shove isn't a good reason for fighting."

"That's right," said Dad as they forged through the crowd back to their car. "If it were, there wouldn't be a person left unscarred at this craft show."

> They shall beat their swords into plowshares, and their spears into pruning hooks.
>
> Isaiah 2:4

Lord, help us to look to your power first.

The Uncool

From the moment he shoved open the car door in the church parking lot, Brent dropped out of the Bradley family. For the next hour or two he would make sure that he stayed clear of his father. Brent waited in the hall for his friends, watching as his dad took a worship folder from the usher and went inside the sanctuary. After a few minutes, Brent realized that none of his friends was going to show up.

He waited until he heard the organ playing the introduction to the first hymn. Then he slipped into one of the back pews next to the wall. He could make his entrance without a sound since he was wearing his soft-soled running shoes. Dad and he had argued about those shoes many times. Dad was one of those stubborn parents who thought it was a sin to wear shoes like that in church. Brent felt proud that his own stubbornness had finally out-lasted his dad's. Why, his dad had not even said a thing about his shoes this morning.

From where he sat he could not see the choir, but he could tell by the voices that some of the kids he knew were singing this morning. The choir director had once told him he had a beautiful voice and asked him to join the choir. "I wouldn't be caught dead singing in a choir," he thought.

While the pastor was reading the announcements, Brent looked out over the faces of the congregation to see who was there that he knew. One of his best friends, Al Richards, was stuck on the end of a row with his parents. From the way he glanced around nervously, Brent could tell that he was embarrassed to be there.

"Poor guy," Brent thought. "No wonder he didn't meet me before the service. Alright! He's wearing his running shoes too."

After the service Brent and Al escaped out the doors as soon as possible. Al was so angry he could hardly wait to get through the doors before saying, "Parents! They don't understand anything! What do they care how stupid I look? How many other guys get stuck sitting with their parents?"

Brent shrugged. "That's the way they are some-times. My dad always wants me to look like a junior businessman. He doesn't know what's 'in' these days, and he doesn't care."

"Is he getting on you about grades?" asked Al. "My folks think that if I don't keep an A average that I'm falling apart. Don't they know what it's like to be the only one in class to have his homework done? How many friends does an A student have?"

"Teachers are the same way," nodded Brent. "You know Mr. Garnett in history; he always calls on me in class. One day he said in front of everyone, 'Brent, you have some good ideas, why don't you participate more in class?' I just sort of rolled my eyes at him. The whole class laughed," he beamed.

The next Saturday the two of them unexpectedly found themselves at church again. They squeezed into the back of the old bus the church had rented for the day. "Imagine wasting a day like this at some retarded picnic," grumbled Brent. "But Dad decides he's going to be a sponsor for the youth, so guess who has to come? I'm sure glad you agreed to come along. I owe you a big favor."

"Aw, it'll get my parents off my back," said Al. "Besides, if we're lucky none of the guys at school will find out that we're spending a Saturday being a pair of goody two-shoes."

"Oh, I brought along a little something that may just help us save our reputations," grinned Brent. He carefully pulled a handful of firecrackers out of his pocket, making certain they were hidden by the back of the seat in front of them. "Think we can find a use for these?" Al's laughter was drowned out by the smaller kids on the bus who were singing some kind of camp song.

When the bus doors opened, a husky, middle-aged man with a handlebar mustache was waiting to greet them. Brent and Al acted bored, snapping the gum in their mouths while the man explained a few things about the people they were about to meet. The two

106

retreated to the end of the line when the group filed into a gymnasium-sized room. Half the room was filled with tables and laughing and shouting people. Scissors, colored paper, and glue seemed to be everywhere. The people hovering around the tables were some of the strangest-looking individuals Brent had ever seen. He nudged Al, and the two of them laughed at some of the clumsier ones.

Suddenly the retarded group noticed the newcomers. Most of them dropped whatever they were doing and charged over, hollering greetings. A boy with a name tag that said "Claude" grabbed Brent by the hand. In broken English the boy asked Brent to follow him. Brent was stunned by the boy's oddly shaped head and wild, flapping style of running. He seemed to be older than Brent, yet he acted like a three year old.

Claude sat behind a table littered with leather scraps and discs. He looked up at Brent with a huge grin. Brent could not help smiling back. He sat down next to Claude and showed him how to make designs on the leather with a punch. Claude's eyes grew wide as he watched Brent take a small rubber hammer and whack the punch. When Brent lifted up the tool, a clear shape of a star was imprinted in the leather. Claude laughed and stuck out his hand to shake hands.

Then he grabbed the hammer himself and tried to do what he had seen Brent do. But his hand slipped, and he managed only a small cut in the leather. Brent offered to demonstrate again, but Claude shook his head with brow furrowed in deep concentration. Claude tried again and again. Some of the

107

time his hand slipped or he missed the punch altogether. But occasionally he was able to make a faint pattern in the leather. After each success he howled with laughter and stuck out his hand at Brent.

"You know what?" said Claude, leaning closer to Brent. "You're cool." The two of them ran across to the open side of the room where Al was bouncing a basketball to two very short boys. By the time they finished throwing the ball around and playing keep-away, it was nearly time to leave. The afternoon had passed quickly.

They all sat down at the tables again, and the man with the large moustache reappeared. "Do any of you know 'Jesus Loves Me?'" he asked.

The roar of yeses nearly echoed off the walls of the room. Brent felt embarrassed as everyone began to sing. But when Claude stared at him with a hurt look, he smiled back and joined in softly. He glanced around to make sure that Al was not watching him. But Al was too busy trying to hold his own in a singing match with the two short boys to notice. When the singing was over there were loud "good-bye's" and "thank you's" from everyone in the room.

Brent felt warm inside as he sat down next to his dad on the bus ride home. "Are you sorry you got dragged along to this?" asked his dad.

"No," Brent answered. "This was really different. It's strange, but after awhile I think I felt more at home with those kids than I usually do with my own friends."

"I'll bet you didn't feel anything like that when you first walked in," said Dad. He noticed that Al was sleeping, his head propped against the bus window.

"No, it took a little while," said Brent. "I think it really hit me when Claude told me I was cool." He grinned at the memory. "It struck me that I wasn't being cool at all. No one was being cool. In fact, I've never seen anyone less cool than Claude. Yet somehow these kids get to you. They make you feel happy and sorry for them at the same time."

"The Bible says that God made what is weak in the world to shame the strong," said Dad. "Maybe he made the 'uncool' to shame the 'cool'."

"It really makes me wonder," said Brent. "Yesterday I would have told you that only a dope would sing 'Jesus Loves Me' at my age. But there wasn't anything silly about it today. Those kids sang it as though they really believed it and weren't ashamed of it a bit."

"Maybe if people weren't so worried about living up to some make-believe ideas of how a person should act we could have more moments like today."

"I guess so," said Brent. "After watching Claude and his friends, I have to say that when we act cool we make ourselves *un*likeable. Just the opposite of what we really want to do. Well, I do know one thing," he said, reaching into his pocket and holding out the contents to his dad. "Firecrackers are 'cool,' and they would have ruined a very important day."

> For every one who exalts himself will be humbled, and he who humbles himself will be exalted.
> Luke 14:11

Sometimes I have to wonder, Lord, who am I try-ing to impress? Anyone can be selfish, uncaring, "cool." So why do I feel I must prove I can be that way too? Help me, rather, to be a warm person.